The Essence of Attitude

Compiled by
Katherine Karvelas
Successories, Inc., Editorial Coordinator

CAREER PRESS
3 Tice Road, P. O. Box 687
Franklin Lakes, NJ 07417
1-800-CAREER-1; 201-848-0310 (NJ and outside U. S.)
FAX: 201-848-1727

THE ESSENCE OF ATTITUDE
Cover design by Successories
Typesetting by Eileen Munson
Printed in the U.S.A. by Book-mart Press

To order this title, please call toll-free 1-800-CAREER-1 (NJ and Canada: 201-848-0310) to order using VISA or MasterCard, or for further information on books from Career Press.

Library of Congress Cataloging-in-Publication Data

The essence of attitude : quotations for igniting positive attitudes / by editors of Successories.

p. cm.
ISBN 1-56414-383-X (pbk.)
1. Attitude (Psychology)--Quotations, maxims, etc.
I. Successories.
BF327.E77 1988
153.8'5--dc21 98-28301

Introduction

The search for personal and professional success is a lifelong journey of trial and error. This inspiring collection of wit and wisdom is a celebration of life's lessons. Each saying is a motivational push to stay on track of your goals and pursue your dreams.

In these pages you will find more than 300 powerful and compelling quotations from a diverse group of people—business professionals, writers, activists, actors, artists, sports professionals, scientists, philosophers, politicians, and everyday people who inspire us.

This unique collection was compiled after years of insightful reading and warm discussions with people who were kind enough to share their personal collections of quotations. Working on this book has been an enlightening and gratifying experience. We hope reading these quotes will be an equally gratifying and motivating experience for you on your journey of success.

How a person masters his fate is more important than what his fate is.

Wilhelm von Humboldt

A positive thought is the seed of a positive result.

Anonymous

So of cheerfulness, or a good temper, the more it is spent, the more it remains.

Ralph Waldo Emerson

In the long run, we get no more than we have been willing to risk giving.

Sheldon Kopp

We are all worms, but I do believe I am a glowworm.

Winston Churchill

To find something you can enjoy is far better than finding something you can possess.

Glen Holm

There is only one corner of the universe you can be certain of improving, and that's your own self.

Aldous Huxley

Positive attitudes create positive people.

Anonymous

Do what's right. Do it right. Do it right now.

B. C. Forbes

K*now the value of time; snatch, seize, and enjoy every moment of it. No idleness, no delay, no procrastination; never put off till tomorrow what you can do today.*

Earl of Chesterfield

As I grow older, I pay less attention to what men say. I just watch what they do.

Andrew Carnegie

Kindness is wisdom.

Phillip J. Bailey

I'm happier. I guess I made up my mind to be that way.

Ralph Waldo Emerson

A problem is a chance for you to do your best.

Duke Ellington

Service is the rent we pay for being. It is the very purpose of life, and not something you do in your spare time.

Marion Wright Edelman

The harder you fall, the higher you bounce.

Anonymous

The glow of one warm thought is, to me, worth more than money.

Thomas Jefferson

If you don't like something, change it. If you can't change it, change your attitude. Don't complain.

Maya Angelou

Happiness is a choice that requires effort at times.

Anonymous

Do continue to believe that with your feeling and your work you are taking part in the greatest; the more strongly you cultivate in yourself this belief, the more will reality and the world go forth from it.

Rainer Maria Rilke

In the long run men hit only what they aim at.

Henry David Thoreau

Wherever you go, no matter what the weather, always bring your own sunshine.

Anonymous

The only limit to our realization of tomorrow will be our doubts of today.

Franklin D. Roosevelt

A positive attitude is a person's passport to a better tomorrow.

Anonymous

The way to overcome shyness is to become so wrapped up in something that you forget to be afraid.

Lady Bird Johnson

A chip on the shoulder indicates that there is wood higher up.

Jack Herbert

No great thing comes to any man unless he has courage.

Cardinal James Gibbons

We are what we think. All that we are arises with our thoughts. With our thoughts, we make the world.

Buddha

Happiness is not a state to arrive at but, rather, a manner of traveling.

Samuel Johnson

People are always blaming circumstances for what they are. I don't believe in circumstances. The people who get on in this world are the people who get up and look for the circumstances they want and if they can't find them, make them.

George Bernard Shaw

Continually strive to improve yourself.

Anonymous

There are things I can't force. I must adjust. There are times when the greatest change needed is a change of my viewpoint.

C. M. Ward

The world is extremely interesting to a positive person.

Anonymous

Don't be afraid to give up the good to go for the great.

Kenny Rogers

Reflect upon your present blessings, of which every man has plenty; not on your past misfortunes, of which all men have some.

Charles Dickens

I praise loudly; I blame softly.

Catherine II

Attitudes are a secret power working 24 hours a day, for good or bad.

Anonymous

If you think you can win, you can win. Faith is necessary to victory.

William Hazlitt

The poor man is not he who is without a cent, but he who is without a dream.

Harry Kemp

Exhilaration of life can be found only with an upward look. This is an exciting world. It is cram-packed with opportunity. Great moments wait around every corner.

Richard De Vos

As a person thinketh so are they.

James Allen

No problem can withstand the power of sustained creative thought.

Anonymous

Life is a grindstone. Whether it grinds us down or polishes us up depends on us.

L. Thomas Holdcroft

Keep your heart right, even when it is sorely wounded.

Anonymous

The most significant change in a person's life is a change of attitude—right attitudes produce right actions.

William J. Johnston

Whether you think you can or you think you can't, you're right.

Henry Ford

Two men look out through the same bars; one sees the mud and one the stars.

Fredrick Langbridge

Trust your hopes, not your fears.

David Mahoney

Whether a glass is half-full or half-empty depends on the attitude of the person looking at it.

Anonymous

To me success means effectiveness in the world, that I am able to carry my ideas and values into the world—that I am able to change it in positive ways.

Maxine Hong Kingston

Worry is the misuse of the imagination.

Anonymous

There are two ways of meeting difficulties: You alter the difficulties or you alter yourself to meet them.

Phyllis Bottome

Don't accept that others know you better than yourself.

Sonja Friedman

Optimism is essential to achievement and it is also the foundation of courage and of true progress.

C. Malesherbez

There is a better way for everything. Find it.

Thomas Edison

Success is dependent on effort.

Sophocles

Knock the *t* off of *can't*.

Anonymous

Just don't give up trying to do what you really want to do. Where there is love and inspiration, I don't think you can go wrong.

Ella Fitzgerald

You must first be a believer if you would be an achiever.

Anonymous

The fountain of content must spring up in the mind, and he who has so little knowledge of human nature as to seek happiness by changing anything but his own disposition will waste his life in fruitless efforts and multiply the grief which he purposes to remove.

Samuel Johnson

There is more to life than increasing its speed.

Gandhi

It isn't hard to be good from time to time in sports. What's tough is being good every day.

Willie Mays

Start every day with an inspiring thought.

Anonymous

Things don't turn up in this world until somebody turns them up.

James Garfield

Promote yourself but do not demote another.

Israel Salanter

We become just by performing just actions, temperate by performing temperate actions, brave by performing brave actions.

Aristotle

A positive attitude is not a destination. It is a way of life.

Anonymous

Above all, challenge yourself. You may well surprise yourself at what strengths you have, what you can accomplish.

Cecile M. Springer

Great things are done more through courage than through wisdom.

German proverb

As novices, we think we're entirely responsible for the way people treat us. I have long since learned that we are responsible only for the way we treat people.

Rose Lane

Little disciplines multiply rewards.

Jim Rohn

The roots of true achievement lie in the will to become the best that you can become.

Harold Taylor

When you're through changing, you're through.

Bruce Barton

You are the sole master of your thought processes.

Anonymous

I don't believe in pessimism. If something doesn't come up the way you want, forge ahead. If you think it's going to rain, it will.

Clint Eastwood

Never trouble another for what you can do for yourself.

Thomas Jefferson

Life is what your thoughts make it.

Marcus Aurelius

Let us think positively and remember that the misfortunes hardest to bear are those which rarely happen.

Anonymous

The first principle of achievement is mental attitude. Man begins to achieve when he begins to believe.

J. C. Roberts

Formulate and stamp indelibly on your mind a mental picture of yourself as succeeding. Hold this picture tenaciously. Never permit it to fade. Your mind will seek to develop the picture. Do not build up obstacles in your imagination. Do not be awestruck by other people and try to copy them. Nobody can be you as efficiently as you can.

Norman Vincent Peale

A man who has to be convinced to act before he acts is not a man of action.

Georges Clemenceau

It's not the situation. It's your reaction to the situation.

Bob Conklin

You cannot always control circumstances, but you can control your own thoughts.

Charles Popplestone

Things turn out the best for the people who make the best of the way things turn out.

John Wooden

Our aspirations are our possibilities.

Anonymous

The difference between a successful person and others is not a lack of knowledge, but rather a lack of will.

Vince Lombardi

No life is so hard that you can't make it easier by the way you take it.

Ellen Glasgow

We can't direct the wind but we can adjust the sails.

Anonymous

Any fact facing us is not as important as our attitude toward it, for that determines our success or failure.

Norman Vincent Peale

Your living is determined not so much by what life brings you as by the attitude you bring to life; not so much by what happens to you as by the way your mind looks at what happens.

John Homer Miller

If you really want to be happy, nobody can stop you.

Anonymous

All life is an experiment. The more experiments you make, the better.

Ralph Waldo Emerson

One cannot control the length of his life, but he can have something to say about its width and depth.

Anonymous

Ability is what you are capable of doing. Motivation determines what you do. Attitude determines how well you do it.

Lou Holtz

The best way to succeed in life is to act on the advice we give to others.

Anonymous

Happiness depends upon ourselves.

Aristotle

What happens to a man is less significant than what happens within him.

Louis L. Mann

Never fear shadows. They simply mean that there's a light somewhere nearby.

Ruth E. Renkei

A new attitude invariably creates a new result.

Anonymous

Don't be discouraged by a failure. It can be a positive experience. Failure is, in a sense, the highway to success, inasmuch as every discovery of what is false leads us to seek earnestly after what is true, and every fresh experience points out some form of error which we shall afterwards carefully avoid.

John Keats

Be not afraid of life. Believe that life is worth living, and your belief will create the fact.

William James

Life was meant to be lived, and curiosity must be kept alive.

Eleanor Roosevelt

Set high standards and few limitations for yourself.

Anonymous

If every day is an awakening, you will never grow old. You will just keep growing.

Gail Sheehy

The strongest principle of growth lies in the human choice.

Anonymous

If you cannot find peace within yourself, you will never find it anywhere else.

Marvin Gaye

No cases of eyestrain have been developed by looking on the bright side of things.

Anonymous

They can conquer who believe they can.

Virgil

Derive happiness in oneself from a good day's work, from illuminating the fog that surrounds us.

Henri Matisse

Keep away from people who try to belittle your ambitions. Small people always do that, but the really great make you feel that you, too, can become great.

Mark Twain

The positive thinker sees the invisible, feels the intangible, and achieves the impossible.

Anonymous

The secret of happiness is to admire without desiring.

F. H. Bradley

We can accomplish many more things if we did not think of them as impossible.

C. Malesherbez

The man with confidence in himself gains the confidence of others.

Jewish proverb

Where there is an open mind, there will always be a frontier.

Charles Kettering

You will only go as far as you think you can go.

Anonymous

As soon as you trust yourself, you will know how to live.

Goethe

He whose face gives no light shall never become a star.

William Blake

The biggest mistake of all is to avoid situations in which you might make a mistake.

Anonymous

Nothing can stop the man

with the right mental attitude

from achieving his goal.

Nothing on earth can help

the man with the wrong

attitude.

Thomas Jefferson

It takes courage to grow up and turn out to be who you really are.

Anonymous

We have survived everything, and we have only survived it on our optimism.

Edward Steichen

Genius is the product of enthusiasm.

Anonymous

Become a fixer, not just a fixture.

Anonymous

Get action. Do things; be sane, don't fritter away your time...take a place wherever you are and be somebody; get action.

Theodore Roosevelt

Simply the thing that I am shall make me live.

William Shakespeare

Everything you can imagine is real.

Picasso

There is no value in life except what you choose to place upon it and no happiness in any place except what you bring to it yourself.

Henry David Thoreau

Give your positive energy a job.

Anonymous

The most important thing about a man is what he believes in the depth of his being. This is the thing that makes him what he is, the thing that organizes him and feeds him; the thing that keeps him going in the face of untoward circumstances; the thing that gives him resistance and drive.

Hugh Stevenson Tigner

Confidence in nonsense is a requirement for the creative process.

Anonymous

Do the right thing. It will gratify some people and astonish the rest.

Mark Twain

Never let the fear of striking out get in your way.

Babe Ruth

Optimists do not wait for improvement; they achieve it.

Paul von Keppler

We must always change, renew, rejuvenate ourselves; otherwise we harden.

Goethe

Use the word "impossible" with great caution.

Anonymous

Determine never to be idle. It is wonderful how much may be done if we are always doing.

Thomas Jefferson

A positive attitude is like a magnet for positive results.

Anonymous

Never discourage anyone who continually makes progress, no matter how slow.

Plato

Twenty years from now you will be more disappointed by the things you didn't do than by the ones you did. So throw off the bowlines, sail away from the safe harbor. Catch the trade winds in your sails. Explore. Dream.

Mark Twain

Have confidence that if you have done a little thing well, you can do a bigger thing well, too.

Anonymous

Do what you know best; if you are a runner, run. If you're a bell, ring.

Ignas Bernstein

Remember the steam kettle!
Though up to its neck in hot water,
it continues to sing.

Anonymous

A positive attitude removes the rust from the mind, lubricates our inward machinery, and enables us to do our work with fewer creaks and groans.

Anonymous

Dreams are renewable. No matter what our age or condition, there are still untapped possibilities within us and new beauty waiting to be born.

Dr. Dale Turner

The last of human freedoms—to choose one's attitude in any given set of circumstances.

Victor Frankl

The only real aging process is the erosion of worthy ideals.

Anonymous

Believe in life! Always human beings will live and progress to greater, broader, and fuller life.

W. E. B. DuBois

Become a possibilitarian.
No matter how dark things
seem to be or actually are,
raise your sights and see the
possibilities—always see them,
for they're always there.

Norman Vincent Peale

Your only obligation in any lifetime is to be true to yourself.

Richard Bach

The art of being happy lies in the power of extracting happiness from common things.

Henry Ward Beecher

Cherish your yesterdays; dream your tomorrows; but live your todays!

Anonymous

Our self-image and our habits tend to go together. Change one and you will automatically change the other.

Maxwell Maltz

Make your life a mission, not an intermission.

Anonymous

The world is what we think it is. If we can change our thoughts, we can change the world.

H. M. Tomlinson

Pride is a personal commitment. It is an attitude that separates excellence from mediocrity.

Anonymous

By your thoughts you are daily, even hourly, building your life; you are carving your destiny.

Ruth Barrick Golden

Nothing is good or bad but that our thinking makes it so.

Shakespeare

If you don't have solid beliefs you cannot build a stable life. Beliefs are like the foundation of a building, and they are the foundation to build your life upon.

Alfred A. Montapert

The mind is its own place, and in itself can make a heaven of hell, or a hell of heaven.

John Milton

A healthy attitude is contagious, but don't wait to catch it from others. Be a carrier!

Anonymous

I have found that if you love life, life will love you back.

Arthur Rubinstein

Happiness is a present attitude—not a future condition.

Hugh Prather

Happy is the man who has broken the chains which hurt the mind, and has given up worrying once and for all.

Ovid

Doubt your doubts, not your beliefs.

Anonymous

Believe that you have it, and you have it.

Latin proverb

There is only one success: to be able to spend your life in your own way, and not to give others absurd maddening claims upon it.

Christopher Morley

All the wonders you seek are within yourself.

Sir Thomas Brown

Life is made up of small pleasures. Happiness is made up of those tiny successes—the big ones come too infrequently. If you don't have all of those zillions of tiny successes, the big ones don't mean anything.

Norman Lear

If I am not for myself, who is for me; and being for my own self, what am I? If not now, when?

Hillel

It's your attitude, not your aptitude, which determines your altitude in life.

Anonymous

They are able because they think they are able.

Virgil

The one thing in the world of value is the active soul.

Ralph Waldo Emerson

Those who give too much attention to trifling things become generally incapable of great things.

Francois de la Rochefoucauld

The positive mind has extra problem-solving power.

Anonymous

Life is an exciting business, and most exciting when it is lived for others.

Helen Keller

Happiness is different from pleasure. Happiness has something to do with struggling and enduring and accomplishing.

Anonymous

Man is only truly great when he acts from his passions.

Benjamin Disraeli

The sincerest satisfactions in life come in doing and not in dodging duty; in meeting and solving problems, in facing facts, in being a dependable person.

Richard L. Evans

The art of life lies in a constant readjustment to our surroundings.

Kakuzo Okakura

Thoughts lead on to purposes; purposes go forth in action; actions form habits; habits decide character; and character fixes our destiny.

Tyron Edwards

If you want to be enthusiastic, act enthusiastic.

Dale Carnegie

Failure is only a temporary change in direction to set you straight for your next success.

Denis Waitley

The one thing worse than a quitter is a person who is afraid to begin.

Anonymous

The real man smiles in trouble, gathers strength from distress, and grows brave by reflection.

Thomas Paine

Happiness is essentially a state of going somewhere wholeheartedly, one-directionally, without regret or reservation.

William H. Sheldon

When we cannot find contentment in ourselves it is useless to seek it elsewhere.

Francois de la Rochefoucauld

Against the assault of laughter nothing can stand.

Mark Twain

I am still determined to be cheerful and happy in whatever situation I may be, for I have also learned from experience that the greater part of our happiness or misery depends on our dispositions and not our circumstances.

Martha Washington

The roots of true achievement lie in the will to become the best that you can become.

Harold Taylor

Happy are those who dream dreams and are willing to pay the price to make them come true.

Anonymous

There are no menial jobs, only menial attitudes.

William Bennett

As long as you live, keep learning how to live.

Seneca

The real winners in life are the people who look at every situation with an expectation that they can make it work or make it better.

Barbara Pletcher

Live every day as if it were your last.

Marcus Aurelius

Do what you can, with what you have, where you are.

Theodore Roosevelt

Our self-image, strongly held, essentially determines what we become.

Maxwell Maltz

You can have anything in life you want if you just help enough other people get what they want.

Zig Ziglar

If you doubt you can accomplish something, then you can't accomplish it. You have to have confidence in your ability and then be tough enough to follow through.

Rosalynn Carter

The way I see it, if you want the rainbow, you gotta put up with the rain.

Dolly Parton

We are what we believe we are.

Benjamin N. Cardozo

Experience often shows that success is due less to ability than to attitude.

Anonymous

Perpetual optimism is a force multiplier.

Colin Powell

Nobody gets to live life backward. Look ahead—that's where your future lies.

Ann Landers

Kind words can be short and easy to speak, but their echoes are truly endless.

Mother Teresa

Self-development is a higher duty than self-sacrifice.

Elizabeth Cady Stanton

Optimism is essential to achievement and it is also the foundation of courage and of true progress.

Nicholas Murray Butler

Nothing in life is to be feared. It is only to be understood.

Marie Curie

The great at anything do not set to work because they are inspired but rather become inspired because they are working. They don't waste time waiting for inspiration.

Ernest Newman

Live your beliefs and you can turn the world around.

Henry David Thoreau

To be truly happy is a question of how we begin, and not how we end, of what we want and not what we have.

Robert Louis Stevenson

Enthusiasm: a little thing that makes a big difference.

Anonymous

Our life is a reflection of our attitudes.

Anonymous

We confide in our strength, without boasting of it; we respect that of others, without fearing it.

Thomas Jefferson

Work is either fun or drudgery. It depends on your attitude. I like fun.

Colleen Barrett

I discovered I always have choices and sometimes it's only a choice of attitude.

Judith M. Knowlton

You are the architect of your personal experience.

Shirley MacLaine

You can't have rosy thoughts about the future when your mind is full of blues about the past.

Anonymous

What a man accomplishes in a day depends upon the way in which he approaches his tasks. When we accept tough jobs as a challenge to our ability and wade into them with joy and enthusiasm, miracles can happen. When we do our work with a dynamic conquering spirit, we get things done.

Arland Gilbert

Enthusiasm finds the opportunities, and energy makes the most of them.

Henry S. Haskins

Positive attitudes create a chain reaction of positive thoughts.

Anonymous

Those who bring sunshine to the lives of others cannot keep it from themselves.

James Barrie

Tough times don't last, tough people do.

Anonymous

Act as if what you do makes a difference. It does.

William James

Believe in what you are doing.

Anonymous

A misty morning does not signify a cloudy day.

Anonymous

True success is overcoming the fear of being unsuccessful.

Paul Sweeny

Become addicted to constant and never-ending self-improvement.

Anonymous

I've never met a person, I don't care what his condition, in whom I could not see possibilities. I don't care how much a man may consider himself a failure, I believe in him, for he can change the thing that is wrong in his life any time he is ready and prepared to do it. Whenever he develops the desire, he can take away from his life the thing that is defeating it. The capacity for reformation and change lies within.

Preston Bradley

Everything you need for a happy life is within yourself.

Anonymous

How wonderful it is that nobody need wait a single moment before starting to improve the world.

Anne Frank

The world hungers for positive attitudes.

Anonymous

My life is my message.

Gandhi

Those who are lifting the world upward and onward are those who encourage more than criticize.

Elizabeth Harrison

Happiness is a direction, not a place.

Sydney J. Harris

Believe the best of everybody.

Rudyard Kipling

There are only two ways to live your life. One is as though nothing is a miracle. The other is as though everything is a miracle.

Albert Einstein

The living moment is everything.

D. H. Lawrence

One essential to success
is that your desire be an
all-obsessing one, your thoughts
and aims be co-ordinate, and
your energy be concentrated
and applied without letup.

Claude M. Bristol

Live your life on purpose.

Dan Zadra

Use what talents you possess. The woods would be very silent if no birds sang there except those that sang best.

Henry Van Dyke

You will rise by lifting others.

Robert Green Ingersoll

Great men are those who find that what they ought to do and want to do are the same thing.

Anonymous

The measure of life is not its duration but its donation.

Peter Marshall

The delights of self-discovery are always available.

Gail Sheehy

Be happy. It's one way of being wise.

Colette

You have to accept whatever comes and the only important thing is that you meet it with the best you have to give.

Eleanor Roosevelt

Goodness is uneventful. It does not flash, it glows.

David Grayson

People are like stained-glass windows. They sparkle and shine when the sun is out, but when the darkness sets in, their beauty is revealed only if there is a light from within.

Elizabeth Kübler-Ross

If you want to be respected, you must respect yourself.

Anonymous

Do a little more each day than you think you possibly can.

Lowell Thomas

The doors we open and close each day decide the lives we live.

Flora Whittemore

Not in time, place, or circumstances, but in the man lies success.

Charles B. Rouss

No man fails if he does his best.

Orison Swett Marden

Joy comes from using your potential.

Will Schultz

There is no such thing as an insignificant improvement.

Anonymous

Give light, and the darkness will disappear of itself.

Desiderius Erasmus

Passions elevate the soul to great things.

Denis Diderot

M*any persons have a wrong idea of what constitutes true happiness. It is not attained through self-gratification but through fidelity to a worthy purpose.*

Helen Keller

Sooner or later, those who win are those who think they can.

Richard Bach

Let nothing dim the light that shines from within.

Maya Angelou

Part of a happy day is refusing to be affected by negative thoughts.

Anonymous

It is not in the stars to hold our destiny but in ourselves.

Shakespeare

The greatest discovery of any generation is that a human being can alter his life by altering his attitude.

William James

Expect to win.

Anonymous

If you are all wrapped up in yourself, you are overdressed.

Kate Halverson

Your mind will give back exactly what you put into it.

Anonymous

Mistakes are the portals of discovery.

James Joyce

However mean your life is, do not blame it; do not shun and call it hard names. It is not so bad as you are. It looks poorest when you are richest. The fault-finder will find faults even in Paradise. Love your life.

Henry David Thoreau

Everyone thinks of changing the world, but no one thinks of changing himself.

Leo Tolstoy

If it is to be...it is up to me.

Anonymous

All the resources we need are in the mind.

Theodore Roosevelt

A person will be just about as happy as they make up their minds to be.

Abraham Lincoln

When fate hands us a lemon, let's try to make lemonade.

Dale Carnegie

A creative attitude is the fuel of progress and growth.

Anonymous

Our attitudes can be the anchor of the soul and the incentive for achievement.

Anonymous

True wisdom lies in gathering the precious things out of each day as it goes by.

E. S. Bouton

Bloom where you are planted.

John D. Rockefeller

Instead of thinking about where you are, think about where you want to be. It takes twenty years of hard work to become an overnight success.

Diana Rankin

When we put a limit on what we will do, we put a limit on what we can do.

Charles Schwab

Whatever you are, be a great one.

Anonymous

Either I will find a way, or I will make one.

P. Sidney

The very act of believing creates strength of its own.

Anonymous

The destiny of man is in his own soul.

Herodotus

The mind moves in the direction of our currently dominant thoughts.

Earl Nightingale

Keep your face to the sunshine and you cannot see the shadows.

Helen Keller

Be assured that any worthwhile action will create change and attract support.

Philip Marvin

Your day goes the way the corners of your mouth turn.

Anonymous

Every great and commanding moment in the annals of the world is the triumph of somebody's enthusiasm.

Ralph Waldo Emerson

What wisdom can you find that is greater than kindness?

Jean-Jacques Rousseau

We don't know who we are until we see what we can do.

Martha Grimes

Success is the positive realization of a worthy goal or ideal.

Earl Nightingale

Don't go through life, *grow* through life.

Anonymous

It's time to start living the life we've imagined.

Henry James

The longer you live the more you realize that forgiveness, consideration, and kindness are three of the great secrets of life.

Anonymous

Be the change you want to see in this world.

Gandhi

The pessimist sees difficulty in every opportunity. The optimist sees opportunity in every difficulty.

Winston Churchill

In the middle of every difficulty lies opportunity.

Anonymous

There is little difference in people, but that little difference makes a big difference. The little difference is attitude. The big difference is whether it is positive or negative.

W. Clement Stone

Let a joy keep you. Reach out your hands and take it when it runs by.

Carl Sandburg

When the past tries to dominate your thoughts, let your dreams ignite your day.

Anonymous

The longest journey of any person is the journey inward.

Dag Hammarskjöld

These other Successories® titles are available from Career Press:

- *The Magic of Motivation*
- *The Power of Goals*
- *Commitment to Excellence*
- *Winning with Teamwork*
- *The Best of Success*